# Collected Poems

by Sylvia Murphy

Collected Poems by Sylvia Murphy

© Sylvia Murphy 2018

Sylvia Murphy has asserted her right under the Copyright, Designs and patents Act, 1988, to be identified as the author of this work.

Cover artwork by KreativeHexenkueche at:
https://pixabay.com/en/users/KreativeHexenkueche-8926/

This book is sold subject to the condition that it shall not by way of trade or otherwise be lent, resold, hired out, or otherwise circulated without the publishers' prior consent in any form of binding or cover than that in which it is published and without a similar condition including this condition being imposed on the subsequent publisher.

**Contents**

Introduction: About the Author

| | |
|---|---|
| ...And Yet... | 1 |
| A Poet Dies | 3 |
| After The Death | 4 |
| An African Road | 5 |
| Answer Me | 6 |
| Apologising | 8 |
| Billy McClusky's Bus | 10 |
| Birthing | 11 |
| Burning The Boat | 12 |
| Elephant Bones | 14 |
| Ending | 15 |
| Estuary | 16 |
| Evening | 17 |
| Feeding | 18 |
| Fell | 19 |
| Granny | 20 |
| Her Shoes | 21 |
| His Shoes | 23 |
| Honeymoon | 24 |
| Killing Time | 25 |
| Ladies of Leisure | 26 |
| Listening To Africa (Where The Nights Are Never Quiet) | 27 |
| Long Time Pass | 28 |
| Make Me A Promise | 29 |
| My Beach | 30 |
| My Old Grey Cardigan | 31 |

| | |
|---|---|
| My PD | 32 |
| My Words | 33 |
| Once I was a Person | 34 |
| Once Palestine | 35 |
| One More Poem | 37 |
| Poems Children Write | 38 |
| Remembering Tuesday | 40 |
| Seminar | 41 |
| Shipmate | 42 |
| Sisters | 43 |
| Solstice | 44 |
| Supermarket Sonnet | 45 |
| The Cat Sits | 46 |
| The Chicken Run | 47 |
| The Children | 48 |
| The Expert | 49 |
| The Fig Tree | 51 |
| The Last Sleep | 53 |
| The Lost Poem | 55 |
| The Masterpiece | 57 |
| Travellers From Another Planet | 58 |
| Water Rules | 59 |
| When I Was A Kid | 61 |
| Where Is It? | 63 |
| Winter | 64 |
| Your Picture | 65 |

## Introduction: About the Author

Although I am now eighty years old, suffering from the effects of advanced Parkinson's Disease and living in a nursing home, I still love to read and write poetry, as I have done all my life.

Alongside a lengthy teaching career in the humanities, such as Sociology and Geography, followed by a period as a School Inspector, I have written, as either Sylvia Greenland or Sylvia Murphy, poetry, fiction and non-fiction.

The numerous books of fiction and non-fiction published include The Complete Knowledge of Sally Fry, The Life and Times of Barly Beach, Tyfoon's Tale, Keeping Nyala In Style, and Candy's Children.

I have had many short stories in popular women's magazines and cat magazines, and lots of poems in periodicals and books published by poetry groups including Ver Poets, Poetry Now and The Poetry Foundation.

Among my own personal favourite poets are Ted Hughes, Bill Greenwell, Sharon Olds, Jack Carey, Simon Armitage and Alice Oswald.

Here in this collection are some of my favourite poems that I've written over the years. I very much hope you enjoy reading them as much as I've enjoyed writing them.

**...And Yet...**

I never, never dream of you – and yet
my drowsing moments, leading up to sleep,
are filled with shadows where I find your face,
and memories of swiftly shuttered looks
that paced the secret measure of your heart
when in unguarded moments you have shown
the unadmitted wakening of love.

I never, ever dream of you – and yet
your presence lingers hourly at my side
and when I need to turn away from you,
to grasp my life, to dull the lonely ache,
I see the shadow in your eyes of pain
that we should part, and your pain echoes mine,
and yet you never told me that you care.

I never need to dream of you because
as I awake it is to thoughts of you,
of whether you are thinking then of me,
imagining the lightness of your touch;
and asking whether you imagine too
and whether you are taken by the fear
that I no longer want to think of you.

I never dream of you at all – thank God!
For if I did there would be no escape,
no place to hide, to call my heart my own.
I welcome sleep, I draw the darkness close
and hope that if tomorrow I should wake

I will no longer see your haunting eyes
or care to wonder if you love me still.

**A Poet Dies**

When a poet dies
A light goes out
In some far off firmament
And the universe shudders

**After The Death**

How does it feel in there,
deep in the clay,
deep and alone?
How does it feel?

How does it move in there,
deep and alone,
deep in the dark?
How does it move?

Is there a stirring of life
deep in the clay?
Deep in the dark with you,
is there a life?

How does it go with you,
asleep and alone?
Deep and alone,
How does it go?

**An African Road**

It isn't hard to believe
that this road has not changed
since Eve first set her feet in the hot dust
outside Eden's gate,
lifted her burden onto her head
and began to walk.

It isn't hard to believe
that, as she gathered her children
and set her face to the pitiless miles,
the sight of the dry red road
etched in the earth
broke her heart.

It isn't hard to believe
that as she trod that first long day
over the tortured land
and heard her children weep,
she did not understand
that her journey would last for ever.

**Answer Me**

Is anyone there?
Is there any chance
Of a word with a human being,
With a voice that can respond
To my questions,
Can understand how it feels
To have a heart
That beats with rage and frustration
At this endless,
Mechanical,
Inane
List of choices that I don't want

Is anyone there?
Is there any chance
Of speaking to a person
Who might have an answer
To my enquiry,
Who might be interested
In the fact
That I don't like the service I'm getting
And I want to know
Something,
Somehow
Not listed by your computer?

Is anyone there?
Is there any chance
Of someone who can hear me,

Who has any control
Over this machine,
Who can press a button
And let me out
Of this mindless mechanical circuit
And give me a simple
Yes or no?

**Apologising**

I'm sorry, I have to apologise,
I am white, female and middle class.
In that order? How can I claim
feeling, suffering, vindication,
when birth and circumstance have set me down
wallowing in largesse of earth's gentle bounty,
pampered and cherished from the start?

I have loved and fucked and birthed in ways
said to be without distinction.
Triumphs and joys have been understood and
                                           understated,
fear trivial, privations minimal,
opportunities for violation and betrayal severely
                                           limited.

Had I been black or brown,
male, deprived or under-funded,
I might have railed against fate,
called on rooftop witnesses to the injustice
of my handicap, denying my fulfilment.

My attempts at self-realisation
would have attained the stature of epics.
But my only serious distress has been knowing
That my failures have no co-authors,
are my own unaided work.
My only struggle has been waged against

acceptance of a privileged order of things,
and I have lost.

**Billy McClusky's Bus**

Billy McClusky is driving the bus –
Not for himself,
for all of us.

Billy McClusky knows the way –
he not only knows where we want to go
but he knows how to get there, day on day.

Never needs glance at the dashboard clock –
knows the time to the nearest tock,
he's Billy McClusky, you see.

**Birthing**

As the quiet evening closes on the plain
I have to ask again,
Is this really love that draws us close?
How can love breed monsters such as this,
Springing from our gently nurtured seeds.
I see that huge head thrusting through the nest you
                                      made,
Oozing flux across the sheet
And punctuated by your birthing scream?

How will we ever learn to love again?

**Burning The Boat**

When we were first together
wrapped in fresh love,
building our life,
I never thought of this.
I never thought of the end.

Yet today I am making a fire
to burn our boat.

I never thought
to smash these boards
that held us safe,
I never thought to watch the flames
consume the wind and the spray.

I never thought to see
that blue paint
blister and lose its substance
in the heat,
or to take the helm
where once our hands rested together
guiding our course,
and use it to stir the fire.

When we were first together
sailing an unknown sea,
I never thought of one day
ripping you up

and feeding you, rib by rib,
into the flames.

**Elephant Bones**

So this is the end of the journey
that started one day
when you dropped,
soft and damp,
into the shade of your mother,
her gentle touch confirming
the arrangement of your bones,
her precious memories already opening your future
like flowers?

So is this the end of the journey
that spanned the globe,
your great feet crossing a hundred
miles a day of desert sands,
memorising a thousand water-holes
in a lifetime of mapping wild roads
in your mind?

So is this the end of your years,
proud matriarch leading your herd
through empty wastes?
Is this the end,
this random pile of bleaching bones
leaching your memories into the moving sand
with every rain that falls,
giving your wisdom back to the earth?

**Ending**

Weep not for me,
because I have departed on a new adventure
and I am already talking and laughing
with old friends
around the campfires of the future.
We will miss each other for a while
but I will wait for you
and when the time comes
we will be together again.

**Estuary**

As far as I can look I see the sea
Awaiting promise of the gentle sight
Of eel-grass swaying in the water at my heels
To wait upon the darkness as it falls
And let it take the gate at water's flood.

**Evening**

The evening comes over the hill,
Carrying on its back
The remains of the day.
Already others have abandoned the work
With careless flippancy
As they try to underpace
Their heavy breath.

Finding the burden of the last hours
Too much to support alone,
The evening takes its long shadow,
Flings itself down
And shatters.

**Feeding**

I'd really like to see you as you were –
a squally babe with dirty clothes to wear –
your food spread out across your face,
impossible to keep in place
as every puce and angry roar
directs towards the sopping floor
the nourishment I laboured to provide
to help you grow to be a source of pride.
Instead this monster of requited hate
has learned to wound me through your dinner plate.

**Fell**

When I walked out to find the spring,
the dew clung tightly to my socks,
icing my feet in place
as I followed the fresh runnels that made their way
                             among the rocks
full of promise to take part in the improvisation
of full-blown rivers.

In summer the days sauntered across the land
blowing before it
rich scents of dust as it organises itself
into whorls of pleasure
when evening promises to carry thunder on
                          clouds too heavy
for the air to trust.
Rivers are forgotten, only torrents.

It's autumn and my hopes are laid aside,
challenged by brambled pathways over-worn,
clutching at my wet and booted feet
as early promise is withdrawn
and sluggish rivers draw me from the land
while I stand still and watch them flow.

Then winter, holding out a hand
wraps me into coming years
in ways I do not want to understand
when it becomes too hard to walk the fells,
too cold, too wet and too much gone downhill.

**Granny**

There's nothing Granny couldn't do
And almost nothing that she doesn't know,
There are places she has been
Which no-one else has seen
And more are waiting when she wants to go.
She visits us when we are home,
To see our projects and correct mistakes.
And if she makes a sponge cake she never
                                        gets it wrong,
And no-one can remember when she
                              overcooked a meal.
She never misses birthdays
And always knows our ages
And takes us out and buys us fancy gear.
She takes us to the swimming pool
And watches football at the school.
She does the quizzes every night
And usually gets the answers right,
Which makes our friends a little bit mad
For other families just don't know
That they should manage Granny, so
We keep her with us
So we can be sure
She likes us passing her around.
She isn't really ours at all,
She's a Granny that we found.

**Her Shoes**

When we tidied her up
after the funeral
she had twenty-seven pairs of black shoes
(some still in their boxes)
and a pair of pink slippers.

Why did she have
so many pairs of black shoes?
We voice our question in awed whispers,
so as not to disturb the past
that lay thick over everything.

We looked at each shoe,
wallowing in the empty time, knowing
that she could not return to ask us
(in that abrasive voice she had)
what we thought we were doing there
going through her things.

Using our imaginations
– by that time running like wild antelope
across the landscape of her life –
we found high-kicking fashion items,
curve of the ankle, lure of the leg shoes.
Had she once been vain enough for those,
she with purple-blotched swollen ankles?

We found teeter-and-stride power shoes
for planting firmly in the faces of the fallen,

and stilettos for serious wounding.
How long since she had been so strong
that she could trample those who tried
to knock her down?

We saw, too, her flat-heeled running
                              for the bus shoes,
her scuffed kneel to weed the garden shoes,
and one pair of diamanté-buckled
                    dance the night away sandals
telling stories we didn't try to listen to.

Only the slippers made sense
            of the person we knew –
bumbling old lady velour slippers,
edged with fur fabric,
and they were useless in the end
because after the gangrene set in
she had no feet.

**His Shoes**

I'd know them anywhere, those shoes,
found stuffed in the back of the wardrobe.
Brown suede lace-ups, toes scuffed to shiny circles,
hinged creases sculpted by half a million steps.

Why has he kept them for so long?

I'd know them anywhere, I learned them long ago,
saw them side by side beside my bed,
patiently waiting
while I opened my sleep-filled eyes,
braced for his touch as he heeled off
first one shoe and then the other.
Sighing as his socks left the floor
and the bed creaked.

Why has he kept them?

Did he know that one day I would find them
and, holding in my hands,
would feel the pain erupt afresh?

**Honeymoon**

I wish could remember how it was
as we glued our yesterdays together
in time's glossy album –
with time's passing
it seems as though we might have been...

...happy?

Smile across the breakfast table,
days allowed to drift in tandem
through the blown sands –
bodies working like magnets
to keep us together – forever.

Yes... yes...
always together.
That tentative touching,
closing the spaces between us.
Didn't we laugh at such togetherness,
trying to imagine
being able to part
after the holiday
had snatched our time away.

I remember it now.
It was as though we could have been... happy?

Yesterday?

**Killing Time**

I hate killing time,
It suffers so much as it dies.

As every hour
Strides bravely to its conclusion
I can see the question in its heart –
"When we are all so precious,
Why was I left by the wayside?"

And each little minute that hurries by
Wonders why
Nobody tries to save them,
Gather them together in tens,
And put them to good use.

Watching the seconds
Dancing along before them,
Too small to make a difference on their own,
The hours weep silently
For the waste of it all.

**Ladies of Leisure**

Every morning about eleven we meet
In one house or another,
It gives us time to take the children to school
And set the daily to her jobs.
Elsie's or Pat's or Susan's, we take it in turns,
Just for coffee and biscuits
(Not if we're going to town of course,
Then we miss out).

Nothing special, you know, just mugs
And biscuits out of the tin,
Except for Saturdays,
Then it's best china and traycloths –
We feel we must keep up some standards.

Bored with the same faces?
Not at all. It's fun.
After all, there's so much to discuss –
Diets, and clothes, and having the house painted up.
And where our husbands will take us out to dine.
And we show off things we've bought.
It's most exciting really,
The time goes very fast.

**Listening To Africa (Where The Nights
 Are Never Quiet)**

What do you hear
when you switch off your mind
and listen for the silence?

Do you hear the wind,
the rhythmic breathing
of the lungs of the world?

Do you hear the tears of your children
feeding mighty rivers
as they sweep the land to the sea?

Do you hear the cries of the newborn
mingled with death,
hunters and hunted never still?

Do you hear the slow throb
of the great beating heart
that never rests?

**Long Time Pass**

Long time pass
since I went to Africa,
where its soft caressing mists
led me along your secret folded ways.

Long time pass
since I swam the Zambezi
in the company of elephants;
since I heard the screams
that filled the nights
and etched the trees against an angry moon.

Is long time since
I gathered in my heart
the brushstrokes of the wilderness
to colour Africa and carry it away.

Now I can only imagine how it is.
Empty spaces where we stood together,
and nothing binding us to Africa.

**Make Me A Promise**

Make me a promise,
borrow confections of images
out of the air.
Spin me a web
that will clothe your intentions with rainbows
and let me have taste of your love.

Make me a promise,
bring me an arm full of flowers
fresh from the rain.
Craft me a tale
that will marry inventions with fancies
and let me engage with your heart.

Make me a promise,
breathe me a kiss on my skin
like mist on the dawn.
Cast me spell
that will sweeten my senses with yearning
and let me be clothed in delight.

Make me a promise,
bring me the gift of your heart
wrapped in shimmering silk.
Weep me a tear
that will wash us a river of passion
and let me come bathe in your love.

**My Beach**

This is the beach of my life,
The littoral of my existence,
Where I have trod my footsteps in time
And watched them swallowed by the hours.

Here I have walked my days away,
Amongst the flotsam of other lives
That have briefly drifted against mine,
Leaving half-buried dreams for me to find.

Here have I left poems in the sand
And watched the hammer of a storm
Smash their alliterations apart
Into a million separate blankets of foam.

Here I have sung with the wind,
Exchanging choruses of grief
That beg for resolution.
This is the beach of my life,
Where I have scattered my elver words carelessly,
Leaving them to write their own story
                        in the moving tide.

**My Old Grey Cardigan**

Tidily folded, uninvited,
You lie in the corner
Ignored and slighted
Day after day.
Yet you still catch my eye,
Tempt me to pause and sigh,
Imagine a further day
Embroidering my skin,
Holding me in,
Together,
A little longer,
Stronger.

Each time something new,
Broken buttons,
Worn out seams,
Ribs unknitting
On either sleeve,
And yet you continue to believe
We can hold each other,
Familiar,
Wearing once more together,
My old grey cardigan.

**My PD**

Out of the corner of my eye
I think I spy
A dream just passing, but maybe not.
My head is peopled with cardboard cut-outs
Pretending to imitate my thoughts,

And I know that soon
I will no longer be needed
To fill the spaces.
I will melt away
Into what should be a future
Trying not to follow,
Begging them to take me too
Wishing I knew
How to stop them.
When!?

None of this is real
Beyond the dark passages
Of my poor, mis-shapen brain
Where I struggle against the pain
Again and again
As stealing my dreams
And knitting my imagination
Into the spaces left
By the unravelling of the personality
I may leave behind.

**My Words**

Use my words if they please you,
gather them up
And treat them kindly.
Organise them gently
into stanzas and verses
and them to become
beautiful.

Use my beautiful words
but use them well,
take my visions and knit them,
carefully,
into new designs,
but understand
that they must be loved
before they become yours,
they must be left alone
to make their own sentences.

**Once I was a Person**

Once I was a person
Ready to go –
Ready to take all the best parts
of myself
and make them into something special
                                      and unforgettable.

Where did it all go?
How did I manage such a neat change of use
between one sleep and another?

## Once Palestine

ANOTHER SAVAGE DEATH adorns our streets
Blood scalds the dust,
Spatters onto blackened, battered
Walls,
The BBC correspondent
Manages a shocked tone yet again –

A Palestinian boy,
They say
Of course, for this is where he lives today.
Mistaken for a sniper as he waits
For his mother to bring him to school

(Who mistakes a satchel for a rifle?)
A collective roar of rage
Rises from the mouth of hell
But no regret is expressed,
For really, who was he?

Just one of those
Who belong nowhere
Hardly worth a reference
In the huge catalogue of violence
That is PALESTINE

Once it was different
Once Palestine
Was a land of citrus, farmers, fishermen,
Where we swam in the sea.

My child's eye recalls
Where anchored ships awaited the golden freight

(Who buys Jaffa oranges these days?)
Russet and yellow nasturtiums
Spilled onto the road from white walled yards

And my mother wearing her neat dark frock.
Reached down a single finger
For me to hold
Lest I fall and bruised myself.

No stones, no guns, no tanks
No screams, no blood, no rage
Fruit and flowers and love, and that
                            was once Palestine.

**One More Poem**

My head is heavy,
weighed down by the pain
of grasping all these poems
that I may never see again.

What happens if
dreaming, I slip and fall
and lose them all?
Will I regret the years
wandering through forests of tears
gathering fresh green words?

Or where do I go when
a tempting glimmer shines through the trees
showing where fresh composition waits?
Will there be time
to stop and re-arrange the fallen ends of lines?

Will there be time to rhyme away the pain?

**Poems Children Write**

Poems children write
unfold like new souls,
each one a widening, wondering eye,
opening a window on the light within,
unfurling a new flower.

Poems children write
shine like fresh-flung stars,
each prick of light
a newly born perception
of how to knit the world in place
with words.

Poems children write
spread landscapes of new metaphors
for our inspection.
Lines are linked by
unselfconscious simile
and the spaces are coloured
with hues of description
that rival Solomon.

Poems children write
die young,
lost in the dragon woods of growing up,
as souls, curling at the edges,
starve into wrinkled yellow beasts
and long-forgotten words are binned
in excess of denial.

Did I write that? it can't be cool
to do such yucky stuff!

**Remembering Tuesday**

What happened on Tuesday?
None of us ever forgot
Or wanted to change the way
It happened

Why? What happened?

Nobody knew
But somebody always remembered,
Though no-one completely knew,
Nobody knew for sure.

**Seminar**

Remember that afternoon?
How it changed everything?
How nervous and oppressed we sat
In that stuffy room?
Each spreading her imagination
As we took turns to use the layers and ideas
Spread out before us, hoping we were spending
Them well
By making important named for ourselves.

Glances sped between us
Challenging, reasoning
As we tried out the effects of fresh, alluring words
That we knew would glide us into fresh,
Dimensions, absolutions

Words ready to make the day
A tour expense -
Words that already knew the way
Then, when I looked across to
The final full stop
I had already decided
I would rather go outside
And learn to sail instead.

**Shipmate**

On the dark ocean
where the black skies
stretched to multiple horizons,
you were there,
helping me peel back
the long layers of night
until we found the day.

In the wild tempests
when the white troopers
towered to the crying crowds,
you were there,
helping me ride the snarling seas
until we found peace.

**Sisters**

Together on the evening step
two white heads nod,
four seamed hands rest,
vallanced eyelids blink with rheumy sighs.

Sister,
do you remember how beautiful I was,
I who made love with Adonis
and many others?
Still I feel their warmth, their fire inside me –
Ah, how they loved me!
Now they are all gone,
and their sons too,
leaving me empty.
But how can you understand,
who were never so loved?

Sister,
do you remember how hard I worked,
I who made this garden,
carrying life in water jars?
Still I rejoice in thrusts of new born shoots –
Ah, how I loved the first green!
Now it shades us both
in our evening hours,
leaving me full.
But how can you understand,
who never made a garden?

**Solstice**

It's the longest day
And another year is apexed,
Making its spike in time
Before it folds away
Into the past.

It's the shortest night
And dusk leans into dawn
With barely time for dreams
To drape their webs
Into the future.

**Supermarket Sonnet**

She fell in the precinct and fractured her skull
and nobody knew who she was.
The manager came and examined her head
and gently agreed that she was quite dead
and nobody knew who she was.
A day or two later the coffin came by
and we all brought stuff and had
                    a good cry (was it enough?).
And we stood outside Sainsbury's for
                                most of that day
because nobody knew who she was.

**The Cat Sits**

The cat sits,
Sliding slowly doorward across the mat,
Occasionally, disconsolately,
She opens narrow eyes
And licks her rain-wet rug of fur
Then sighs,
Shutting out the wind
That smears her cold and rheumy nose.
She waits
And waits
And waits some more
Hoping somebody will pass
Who knows
How to open the bloody door.

**The Chicken Run**

Tonight you weren't there
And the people sounded like chickens
And time hung bare
Stretching in endless loops across the evening,
For ever and ever without you.

**The Children**

Oh yes, I remember the children,
They used to run about
On little stubby legs.
I think they had two each,
To keep their balance.
Surely, two apiece was not enough?

They would wave their arms about,
Pretending they could swim in air.
And how they laughed to see
Great clumsy creatures such as you and me
Toppling over in the mud.

**The Expert**

He talks beguilingly of times we left behind,
of finance and success.
He talked about the super-banks,
quite sure he understood the mess
because he'd done it all before
and absolutely knew the score
and knew just what it meant to us.

He talked of plans he'd given us
when sickly traders cried,
and where to turn when credit lines went sour,
reminding us days when greed
must be returned with interest.
He talked of seeking memories of our past
when gain was only earned through pain.

He told us, too, of wealthy office chars,
of making banks look lean
and using cheap largesse that came our way
to scrub the ledgers clean.

He told of days when each was king,
when banks would recognise our wings
and when the money grew too fast too cheap
he taught us other tricky things.

He anecdoted warm and mutual days
when dealers all purported to believe
they understood very clever ways

to float accounts as needed by their friends.
And now we wait out in the cold
and sing
our sad refrain again and yet again.
There's too much money, honey,
too much cash
to stash and trash, then burn instead of earn.

**The Fig Tree**

Hot empty sky,
hot dry wind,
hot earth baking underfoot and lifting dust.
Hot buzzing flies,
cicadas craking everlasting.
Hot, hot, hot afternoon.

On a couch a woman langours,
body damp and misted eyes,
clinging clothes,
thinking of the fig tree by the well.
Thinking of the cool, deep damp,
the deep and shady, leafy cool,
where the pendicles of purple fruit hand poised,
ready, waiting.

The woman rises,
moves with steady pace across the courtyard,
stops before the tree.
Brown arms stretch to part the foliage
and make a way.
She passes through the veil
and branches fold her like caressing arms,
lovers' arms.

Hands reach through to pick, one fruit, two
 and more.
Torn from their shoots they bleed an opiate juice
that falls in slow white drops,

seeping through fingers onto shoulders, breasts.
Cradled by the tree her white teeth split
the purple bursting skin.
Lips suck at pink-fleshed seeds,
tongue pulls the sweet white juice,
drawing life sap from the tree.

Passing by,
as pleases him on hot afternoons,
her suitor wonders why
a serpent came to Paradise
when God made the fig tree long before
to pleasure her.

**The Last Sleep**

Who are all these people
shadowing my pillow,
grey shapes between my fading eyes
and the last of the light,
blanketing my view of tomorrow?
Who are they, approaching in turn
to sigh down on me
then glide away whispering, shaking heads,
voicing my secrets around?
Do I know them?

Whose are these hands
intruding my flesh, smoothing my tangled hair,
gentling my cheeks as they wait
for the time to cradle me away
into the dark?
Whose is this cloying touch,
this Judas caress fluttering,
waiting to close my eyes
for the last sleep?
Do they know me?

Whose are these voices
sneaking through the forests of my mind
with siren calls, ducking behind trees
as I turn to catch their words?
They hound me towards the river where
I will leap into the current
and struggle again upstream, defying Charon,

until the water will swallow me whole,
then spew me out into a place
beyond their reach.

**The Lost Poem**

Nobody knew what it was or where
                               it had come from.

A shapeless sort of thing, it came
one dark and dimpsy day and sat,
and watched them going in and out.
From time to time it reached a hand
and tweaked a hem or shoelace, but
we hurried past, each one of us,
too busy even for a smile
to pass out lips,
to give the thing
a moment of ourselves.

Unhappy, it began to fade,
to lose its meaning and its form,
despairing, curling up to wait for death.
Out of the corner of the my eye
I saw how much it suffered, and
I couldn't leave it crying there alone,
so I picked it up and took it in
and cradled it beside the fire
and watched it as it changed.

The little thing sat soaking up
the warmth of my attention,
becoming whole and beautiful.
I helped it smooth its cadences
and re-arrange its ruffled rhymes

and other curious people stopped and watched.
"What have you got there?" someone asked.
"I'm not sure," I said, "but it looks to me
as though I've found a poem."

**The Masterpiece**

I saw the Mona Lisa today.
She was safely stored and humidified,
adored and suffocating from the press.
Beloved captive in an airtight cage
sheltered from light and cold,
growing old, yet perfectly preserved.

Wearily, enigmatically,
she waited for the crumbling of time,
for air once more upon her hallowed face,
bringing to my eyes
a unique vision of decay.

Her flesh too will wither from the bone,
her hair will shred and fall.
Her crabbed and clasping hands will clutch like claws,
and the smile,
the turn of lip,
that captured a civilisation,
will be a toothless gap.

Then I shall turn my gaze away
and will lie in the same clay.

**Travellers From Another Planet**

No village was marked on the map,
we came upon them unexpectedly.

They must have seen us from miles away,
our truck making a spiral of dust
hovering above the road.

They must have heard us for half an hour,
our engine bellow breaking the still air
and echoing across the veldt.

Gathered by the roadside,
they composed their faces into smiles
and waited for us to pass.

Leaning on their tools, their old bicycles,
they held aloft their melons,
hoping we might stop and buy,

yet knowing really that we would only give them
a wave and continue a journey
that none of them could even comprehend.

The only truck to pass for days,
we came from over there and disappeared that way
leaving a rush of suspense in the air.

We might as well have come from another planet.

**Water Rules**

Planet Earth.
Four-fifths of the surface covered by water –
not just shallow pools
but raging depths that swallow cities,
conceal mountain ranges, fiery eruptions,
and monsters that have never seen light.

How can the inhabitants live with such uncertainty?

Planet Earth.
Atmosphere ninety percent moving vapour
relentlessly sucked from the oceans
and hurled onto the land
in a closed cycle of vomiting hurricanes
tearing out towns and mountainsides.

How can the inhabitants prevail against such force?

Planet earth.
Home to a species composed of two-thirds water,
held together by skin and skeleton.
How do they live,
when flood invades the landscapes year on year,
pitilessly wiping out great swathes of civilisation
in a few seasons?

How can they survive such a regime?

Planet Earth?

Pass it by.
Find somewhere hospitable to settle.

**When I Was A Kid**

When I was a kid the world was round
and I knew where everything was.
The moon stayed in the sky,
always keeping just one step ahead.
There was no television sending out
complicated messages and I listened
to Dick Barton saving everybody on the wireless.
Films were black and white, not shades of grey
and the difference between goodies and baddies
                                        was plain –
goodies wore white and baddies wore black
(and for a while were usually Germans)
and there were no nasty surprises,
                                        no twists in the tail.
Pavements were litter-free because there was
not so much stuff to throw away and you were lucky
if you were born pretty because it was not so easy
to buy good looks in a surgeon's clinic.
Telephones were black and firmly fixed
in draughty corridors. Computers the size of houses
only belonged to universities which most people
never went inside of. Trains huffed and chuffed
and cars broke down a lot but it didn't matter
because not many people had one of those.
There were no iced lollies either, but a penny
                                        would buy
a chocolate ice cream wafer from the
stop-me-and-buy-one man. No refrigerators
kept food fresh at home so housewives

had to go shopping every day which gave them
something important to do.

I wore a blue coat to help my father lay
the lawn outside our new house, and plant
                              the hedge.
Later he went away and I grew up.

**Where Is It?**

Where is it?
Where has yesterday gone?

I left it somewhere,
meaning to come back and use it properly,
but of course
it didn't wait and by the time
I found if again
it was already wandering around
in tomorrow.


All I can do now is go back
to the beginning
before I, too, forget.

**Winter**

I remember Spring,
the waking earth,
the warming of the air,
the rising evening light.

I remember how it feels.

I remember Spring,
the swelling buds,
the tiny creatures born,
the birdsong in the dusk.

I remember how it sounds.

I remember Spring,
the golden dawns,
the greening of the land,
the colours of the flowers.

I remember how it looks.

I remember Spring,
the rising joy,
the pounding heart,
the aching call of love.

Now that Winter calls
I remember how it was.

**Your Picture**

Will you give me that picture? –
The one that you finished today
As I watched how you managed its image,
Each stroke of the brush a tender caress
As you loved it to life of its own.

Printed in Great Britain
by Amazon